THE PATH TO PARADISE

PARADISE

FAITH WISDOM HOLINESS

GEORGE E PFAUTSCH

authorHOUSE®

AuthorHouse™
1663 Liberty Drive
Bloomington, IN 47403
www.authorhouse.com
Phone: 833-262-8899

Published by AuthorHouse 06/21/2023

ISBN: 979-8-8230-1075-7 (sc)
ISBN: 979-8-8230-1076-4 (e)

Library of Congress Control Number: 2023911511

Print information available on the last page.

Scriptural passages have been taken from The New American Bible - St. Joseph Edition and all catechetical passages have been taken from the Catechism of the Catholic Church.

This book is printed on acid-free paper.

CONTENTS

HOLINESS

INTRODUCTION

Surveys indicate that approximately 80 percent of the world's population believe in an afterlife. It is also the belief of most religions of the world that there is some form of afterlife. The belief in an afterlife is founded on faith. We do not have earthly proof that an afterlife exists.

We should respect people of all faiths. Faith is generally based on beliefs learned at an early age and we should appreciate others' faith in their beliefs. We have no reason to believe that people of other faiths are any less sincere or fervent than we are in our own. Having said that, it is perfectly acceptable to proclaim our own faith. That is one of the obligations of my own Catholic faith.

Slightly over 50 percent of the world's population belong to either Christian, Hindu, or Buddhist religions. In addition to an afterlife, many of those belonging to the Hindu or Buddhist religions also believe in some form of reincarnation.

My knowledge of the faith of members in non-Christian religions is limited and this book will therefore deal with the belief of those who are Christians and more specifically with those who are Catholics. Of the world's population, almost one-third belong to some form of Christian religion.

It is a Christian belief that the afterlife will be a life that extends throughout eternity. Because afterlife is an eternal existence, it would seem that a large percentage of people would want to understand more of that existence and adhere to what is necessary to achieve the best place in life hereafter. Sadly, all humans are flawed humans, and the attractions of earthly matters is a distraction from greater emphasis on eternal life.

In our country during the past 50 to 60 years, the percentage of people participating in their Catholic faith has been on the decline. Does that decline foretell us what eternal life may have in store for those who do not participate in their religion? The answer to that is in the hands of our Creator, but we will spend some time looking at that issue, because religious practices can be an important tool in our earthly journey to the afterlife and especially in our journey to Paradise. It was Jesus Christ himself who founded the Church and the important role the Church plays in "The Path to Paradise" should not be ignored.

When I began this book, it was difficult to decide whether the title should be "A Path to Paradise" or "The Path to Paradise". I finally chose the latter, because this book encompasses my personal and somewhat specific views for the Path that is appropriate for me. That does not imply that the Path I detailed in this book is the only Path. During His time on earth our Lord taught us many Truths and it would be presumptuous on my part to think my Path is the only Path for all.

Nevertheless, it is my belief that all Paths to Paradise must include observance of the two great commandments He gave us. We must love Him with all our heart, soul, mind and strength and we must love our neighbor as ourselves. Those are basic to all Paths that lead to Paradise.

This book is divided into three sections: Faith, Wisdom, and Holiness. Each of those are important to the role we seek in eternity.

FAITH

CHAPTER 1

PLANTING THE SEEDS OF FAITH

When we were baptized, we were granted membership in our Church. Our Catholic Church also tells us that "through baptism we are freed from sin and reborn as sons of God." Baptism is a precious gift from God. It is an early grace in our lives.

As soon as possible, it is important to build upon that early grace. It is my belief that one of the biggest reasons that the participation in the Catholic faith has diminished is due to the lack of planting the early seeds of faith in our youth.

Much of the decline in participation of the Catholic faith has occurred in the past 50 to 60 years. Many today blame the sexual abuse scandals within the Church for the decline. I believe that other factors are as much or more to blame for that decline.

In my youthful years (1940's) the tenets of the Catholic faith were not only taught in our homes but were reinforced through religious education in Catholic schools. Members of religious orders were frequently the teachers of such education. For those who were Catholics but could not attend Catholic schools, religious education was provided at some non-school time during the week and often by the nuns who also taught it in the schools. The primary teaching vehicle was the Baltimore Catechism. Those seeds of faith were important.

It is true that faith cannot be taught but the beliefs of our faith can. Teaching those beliefs at an early stage in life makes it much more likely that those seeds of faith will take root at an earlier age.

Because faith is a mysterious and individualistic grace from God, it is my belief that the internal seeds of faith that are planted early have more to do with individualistic growth in faith than do the external sexual abuse scandals or other external factors. History has repeatedly shown that faith has been present for individuals when surrounded by people of no or little faith.

But St. Paul also explained very well that we cannot expect people to believe matters of faith which they have not been taught. It is important to plant the seeds of faith on good soil early in the lives of individuals.

I do not expect all readers of this book to accept my premise on why Church attendance has diminished but I will continue to hold those beliefs until they are proven wrong. The Church today needs a more systematic method of teaching the tenets of our faith.

It is my long-held view that the demise of the Baltimore Catechism without an adequate replacement was a mistake. It took almost 25 years after the use of the Baltimore Catechism was eliminated as the primary teaching vehicle for the Church to issue a new "Catechism of the Catholic Church". Even after its issuance there has not been a compendium prepared for teaching the early elementary grades. That is a flaw which needs to be corrected.

It is not likely that there will be a resurgence of members of religious orders in the near future that will provide Catholic teaching and that is all the more a reason to at least have a Catechism that will provide standard teaching. If and when a Catechism for youths is prepared for teaching, every Bishop in every Diocese needs to instruct all Parishes that such a Catechism is to be used for teaching the Catholic faith.

Bishop Barron, who has served as Chairman of the USCCB (United States Conference of Catholic Bishops) Committee on Catechesis and Evangelization acknowledged that the lack of participation in the Catholic faith is due to a lack of understanding Catholic Doctrine along with teaching that does not correctly portray Catholic teaching.

Recently the USCCB has established an "Institute of the Catechism." If used extensively by those who teach the Catholic faith it can be helpful. But of greater importance is the preparation of a compendium of the

Catechism of the Catholic Church for teaching early elementary grades and the instruction from Bishops that it be used by all Parishes.

At the present time the participation in the Catholic faith continues to diminish. It may well be that other factors beyond a systematic teaching of the Catholic faith contribute to the lack of participation. They can all be addressed once the Church puts in place a systematic teaching of the faith. It is very difficult to address such other factors if the basic teaching of faith is not improved.

Without proper teaching of faith, we are depriving our younger generations of the knowledge of the important steps they need to understand the Path to Paradise. That Path is a path that leads to peace, happiness, and tranquility in the life of those who wish to find the purpose of life.

CHAPTER 2

FAITH

We know that faith is a mysterious and individualistic trait of human beings. It may well relate more to the soul than to the body of humans. That being the case, how can we speak of faith?

Webster's New World Dictionary's initial definition of faith is the "unquestioning belief that does not require proof or evidence." A second definition goes on to define faith as the "unquestioning belief in God, religious tenets, etc."

Those definitions are good but are quite broad. That is probably necessary because there is mystery involved with faith and it is difficult for anyone to assess the faith of another person. Among Christian religions, the Nicene Creed comes as close as we can probably get to assessing the faith of those who are Christians.

It is worth repeating that Creed (Profession of Faith)

before delving much deeper into the mystery of faith. This Profession of Faith is said at many Catholic Masses.

"I believe in one God, the Father almighty, maker of heaven and earth, of all things visible and invisible.

I believe in one Lord, Jesus Christ, the Only Begotten Son of God, born of the Father before all ages, God from God, Light from Light, true God from true God, begotten, not made, consubstantial with the Father: through him all things were made, For us men and for our salvation he came down from heaven, and by the Holy Spirit was incarnate of the Virgin Mary, and became man.

For our sake, he was crucified under Pontius Pilate, he suffered death and was buried, and rose again on the third day in accordance with the Scriptures. He ascended into heaven and is seated at the right hand of the Father. He will come again in glory to judge the living and the dead and his kingdom will have no end.

I believe in the Holy Spirit, the Lord, the giver of life, who proceeds from the Father and the Son, who with the Father and the Son is adored and glorified, who has spoken through the prophets.

I believe in one, holy, catholic, and apostolic Church. I confess one Baptism for the forgiveness of sins, and I look forward to the resurrection of the dead and the life of the world to come. Amen."

There is much mystery and faith contained in the Nicene Creed. It is easy to become so accustomed to reciting the words that we forget to dwell on them as our profession of faith. It is important for all of us to understand what it is we are professing. We will spend the rest of this chapter trying to explain what we are stating as our faith beliefs.

We are taught at an early age that the purpose of life is to know, love and serve God and thereby prepare ourselves for an eternal afterlife of bliss with Him in Paradise.

We begin the Nicene Creed by stating "we believe." The depth to which we believe is up to each of us. We continue by saying we believe that God the Father is almighty. We also believe that He is the creator of heaven and earth as well as all things that are visible or invisible. Implied in that belief is that He created from nothing. The recognition that He is almighty means all things are possible for Him.

All too often humans have attempted to place limitations on His omnipotence with views on "big bang" "evolution" etc. The acceptance of his omnipotence is an important aspect of our faith. Nothing is impossible for our Almighty Father.

As we have listed the Nicene Creed earlier in this chapter, the 2nd and 3rd paragraphs relate to our Lord and Savior, Jesus Christ. There is much to ponder in those two paragraphs. To fully appreciate the miracles and mysteries surrounding our Lord, it is necessary to fully accept that which we profess of Him in the Nicene Creed.

The Catechism of the Catholic Church dedicates pages 106 through 178 to more fully explain the words recited in the above-noted two paragraphs of the Nicene

Creed which relate to our Lord and Savior. To those readers who wish to understand the professions more fully they make in those two paragraphs, I recommend reading those seventy-two pages of the Catechism.

It is natural that more of our Lord and Savior, Jesus Christ, is disclosed to us because he became a human and walked among us. Without his passion and death on a cross, there would be no Path to Paradise. By his death and resurrection, he opened the Kingdom of God for us, so we might one day be with Him in Paradise. During His time on earth, He was also our spiritual teacher and taught us the commands we must follow to obtain a place in Paradise.

After we profess our faith in Jesus Christ, the Creed goes on to note the third person of the Blessed Trinity, the Holy Spirit. The Holy Spirit plays an important role in the daily lives of human beings. By His presence within us, He effectively is our divine Spiritual Director. It is the Spirit's presence, who guides us to spiritual truth. Before Jesus left earth, He told us the Spirit would be with us to guide us spiritually.

The remainder of the Nicene Creed is self-explanatory. We profess the belief in the tenets of our Church and if we are repentant, God forgives us our sins. Finally, we state that we look forward to our eternal life.

These professions of our faith cannot be proven and hence we believe what we profess as a matter of our faith.

Faith is a virtue of most people on earth. As noted

at the beginning of the Introduction, 80 % of people on earth believe in an afterlife. Those who believe that belong to a variety of religions. Just as we firmly believe in the tenets of our own religion, it is important to respect the belief of those who belong to different religions. They too have faith in what they believe.

CHAPTER 3

DEGREES OF FAITH

As noted earlier, faith is both a mystery and very individualistic. It is impossible for one human being to judge the faith of another human being. The depth and sincerity of our faith will be a judgment made solely by our Creator and will determine our place in life hereafter. As a Christian and member of the Catholic Church, I believe very firmly in the teachings of Sacred Scripture as well as the tenets of the Catholic Church. For me, that belief is a necessity to help me grow in faith, wisdom, and holiness. I cannot judge how deeply those beliefs are relative to others.

We do know that during His time on earth, Our Lord, gave us parables to indicate that there are different degrees of faith. He also indicated the depth of faith of various people with whom He had contact. That does tell us that there are varying degrees of faith and that acceptance of "The Truth" is important for us to be able to grow in our faith. When we are baptized, our sponsors profess our beliefs of faith on our behalf. As we gain the use of reason and grow older, it is up to each of us to grow in our faith.

To aid us in growing faith, it is important that our parents, teachers, and catechists inform us of the tenets of our faith. Once we have that knowledge, it is up to each of us to deepen our understanding of those tenets and practice them to the best of our ability.

At the present time in the history of our Church, there has been a sad decline in the participation of our Catholic faith. As already noted, it is my belief that the lack of a systematic approach to teaching our youth the tenets of their faith is the major reason for the subsequent lack of participation.

If and when the Church improves teaching of the faith to our youth and that teaching properly informs our youths of "The Truth" contained in Sacred Scripture and the Catechism, it is up to every individual to grasp that faith and deepen that faith throughout their life.

The degree to which people accept and grow their faith varies. As humans, it is not possible to assess the faith of others, but through Sacred Scripture our Lord has told us that such variance exists.

In Matthew 13 Jesus told the parable of the Sower: *A sower went out to sow. And as he sowed, some seed fell on the path, and the birds came and ate it up. Some fell on rocky ground where it had little soil. It sprang up at once because the soil was not deep, and when the sun rose it was scorched, and it withered for lack of roots. Some seed fell among the thorns, and the thorns grew up and choked it. But some seed fell on rich soil, and produced fruit, a hundred or sixty or thirtyfold. Whoever has ears ought to hear.*

In that parable God is the Sower and the seed is the Word of God. Jesus went on to explain the parable as follows: *The seed sown on the path is the one who hears the word of the kingdom without understanding it, and the evil one comes and steals away what was sown in his heart. The seed sown on rocky ground is the one who hears the word and receives it at once with joy. But he has no root and lasts only for a time. When some tribulation or persecution comes because of the word, he immediately falls away. The seed sown among the thorns is the one who hears the word, but then worldly anxiety and the lure of riches choke the word and it bears no fruit. But the seed sown on rich soil is the one who understands it, who indeed bears fruit and yields a hundred or sixty or thirtyfold.*

If we wish to stay on the path which leads to Paradise, we need to be among those who understand the word of God and act accordingly. In order to do that it is important to accept the word of God as Truth. When we do not accept the word as Truth, it is easy to be among those who do not bear fruit. When we accept his Word as Truth, we can begin the process of growing our faith.

Before we address the ways in which we can grow our faith, let us spend some time on those to whom the seed has not grown on fertile ground. Many in this world deny the existence of God (atheists). It is difficult to believe that people can claim there is no God because of all the physical evidence to the contrary. St. Paul in his letter to the Romans effectively said the same thing,

"For what can be known about God is evident to them, because God has made it evident to them. Ever since the creation of the world, his invisible attributes of eternal power and divinity have been able to be understood and perceived in what he has made." To deny God's existence is the absence of any spiritual wisdom.

Others, as our Lord noted in his Sower parable, have chosen not to grow their faith. For them we should offer our prayers so they may return to accept his Word.

Let us now return to the degrees of faith. Our Lord acknowledges those degrees inasmuch as he says that those who accept the Word bear fruit, with yields of a hundred, sixty or thirtyfold. It should be our goal to be among those who bear a hundred-fold.

The Lord gave us our Church to help us reach that goal. Through the Church the Lord provided the Mass and the Eucharist to permit us to be close to Him during our time on earth. If we wish to be among those who return a high yield of fruit, we will also want to be among those who appreciate his Real Presence in the Eucharist. "Unless you eat of my Body and drink of my Blood you cannot have life within you."

During his time on earth our Lord gave us numerous examples of those He considered to be of great faith as well as examples of those who did not have great faith.

It is good for all of us to remember what Jesus had to say to the chief priests and elders regarding faith in Matthew 22: 31-32: *Amen, I say to you tax collectors and prostitutes are entering the kingdom of God before you. When*

John came to you in the way of righteousness, you did not believe him; but tax collectors and prostitutes did.

Jesus during His time on earth gave us many examples of the value of belief in his Word (The Truth). All of us need to be careful not to judge those among us whom we may view as not being faithful to his Word. Degrees of faith exist among humans and only He will be the one to judge the depth of one's faith.

As we move on to look at the examples Jesus provided us of those who had great faith, one can say that in all cases He made such assertions to those who believed and recognized the reality of his deity.

Let us look at the example of the centurion who approached Jesus as He was entering Capernaum and appealed to Him: *Lord, my servant is lying at home paralyzed, suffering dreadfully. He said to him, "I will come and cure him. The centurion said in reply, "Lord I am not worthy to have you enter under my roof; only say the word and my servant will be healed. For I too am a person subject to authority, with soldiers subject to me. And I say to one, 'Go,' and he goes; and to another, 'Come here', and he comes; and to my slave, 'Do this,' and he does it." When Jesus heard this, he was amazed and said to those following him, "Amen, I say to you, in no one in Israel have I found such faith.*

We know practically nothing of the centurion in whom Jesus found such great faith. We know he was a person of significant authority, but despite that he humbled his own authority to the divine powers of Jesus. He also recognized the reality of the deity of our Lord. In his way he believed deeply in The Truth. He believed in and understood the divine powers Jesus possessed. He was a Roman and a Gentile, but it was his faith that Jesus found exemplary. It is a lesson to us that judgments of faith need to be left in the hands of our Savior.

In the following chapter of Matthew, we are told the story of the curing of the paralytic as he entered his own town: *And there, people brought to him a paralytic lying on a stretcher. When Jesus saw their faith, he said to the paralytic, "Courage, child, your sins are forgiven." At that, some of the scribes said to themselves, "This man is blaspheming." Jesus knew what they were thinking, and said, "Why do you harbor evil thoughts? Which is easier to say, 'Your sins are forgiven,' or to say, 'Rise and walk'? But that you may know that the Son of Man has authority on earth to forgive sins" – he then said to the paralytic, "Rise pick up your stretcher, and go home." He rose and went home.*

In this example of our Lord's divine power, He not only demonstrates his power to work the miracle of curing the paralytic, but also indicates that He was able to forgive sins. In this parable, we are also given the message of the importance of faith. Those who brought the paralytic to Jesus demonstrated great faith, while the scribes disbelieved.

We could cite a number of other examples of Jesus demonstrating his divine powers to those with great faith – the healing of the woman who had bled for twelve years – the curing of lepers, -- restoring sight to the blind – and others, but we will conclude this chapter by looking at two additional Scriptural passages where

Jesus provides us the importance and power of faith. All of these examples imply that there is a difference in the depth of our faith.

We will conclude this chapter with those two Scriptural passages that provide somewhat different messages from Jesus regarding the depth of our faith.

In Luke 18, Our Lord gave the parable of the Pharisee and the Tax Collector." *Two people went up to the temple area to pray; one was a Pharisee and the other was a tax collector. The Pharisee took up his position and spoke this prayer to himself, 'O God, I thank you that I am not like the rest of humanity—greedy, dishonest, adulterous—or even like this tax collector. I fast twice a week, and I pay tithes on my whole income. But the tax collector stood off in a distance and would not even raise his eyes to heaven but beat his breast and prayed, 'O God, be merciful to me a sinner.' I tell you, the latter went home justified, not the former; for everyone who exalts himself will be humbled, and the one who humbles himself will be exalted."*

This parable contains the very strong message of the importance of humility to our faith. It also gives us the message that repentance too is important.

We conclude this chapter with a message on faith from Chapter 17 of Luke. *And the apostles said to the Lord, "Increase our faith." The Lord replied, "If you have faith the size of a mustard seed, you would say to this mulberry tree, 'Be uprooted and planted in the sea, 'and it would obey you.* Whenever we believe we have reached the pinnacle of faith, it is well to remember this message from our Lord.

We have used a number of examples in this chapter to indicate that degrees of faith exist. This writer is not capable of making judgments as to what is entailed with the various degrees but can only say that unless we can move that metaphorical mulberry tree, we need to keep working at increasing our faith.

CHAPTER 4

THE APEX OF FAITH

As I was beginning this chapter, I researched what other writers viewed to be the apex of faith. As is easy to understand, there were many different views. As flawed humans, we are probably not capable of judging the apex of faith and such a definition is probably only in the understanding of our Lord. Since we cannot assess our own faith relative to others, we also cannot assess when we reach the apex.

We do, however, have examples of human beings, who were blessed with great faith. Therefore, we will use those examples to provide the reader with some of the blessings of grace granted to people of great faith.

We will begin with the Blessed Virgin Mary, the mother of God. She had the greatest of blessings when she was conceived without sin. That alone makes her unique among all human beings and also provides us with a model to follow as we attempt to reach the apex of our own faith.

Although our knowledge of the life of the Blessed Mother is limited, we are provided sufficient examples of her life for us to attempt to emulate. When the angel Gabriel announced to her that she was to be the Mother of God, and despite her questioning how this could be since she had no relations with a man, she answered "Thy will be done." Once we profess our faith in God, we have no better words to follow than "thy will be done." If, in our life, we were able to achieve that at all times we would be near the apex of faith, but we are flawed sinners.

Our Blessed Mother undertook much in her life to provide us with examples of the sacrifices we can make to reach the heights of faith. She gave birth in a stable and shortly thereafter had to flee to Egypt in order to protect the life of her Son. She lived in that foreign country for a number of years.

During our Lord's passion and death, she was with Him throughout his ordeal. It must have been an agonizing experience, but one she was willing to endure. Her whole life was a life dedicated to doing the will of God. If we have doubts about the ways we can grow our faith, we have no better model than His Blessed Mother. But our ability to replicate the faith of our Blessed Mother is limited by the fact that she was born without sin.

Another human being who was an example of great faith was John the Baptist. Even before he was born and while in the womb of his mother, Elizabeth, he jumped for joy when Mary, who was pregnant with Jesus came to visit. In the canticle of his father, Zechariah, at the time of John's presentation in the temple, he told all the world that "You my child shall be called the prophet of the Most High and will go before the Lord to prepare His Way." Throughout his life, John would fulfill those words.

The preaching of John had much to do with the necessity of repentance to gain forgiveness of our sins. He, himself, lived a humble life in which he wore simple clothing and ate locusts. But before he died, he also indicated his humanity, inasmuch as he sent messengers to Jesus to explain if He truly was the Messiah. What we can learn from John is the importance of repentance and humility, which are necessary to achieve our apex of faith.

As great as John the Baptist was in his faith, our Lord noted that flawed humans are limited in the faith they can reach during their life on earth. This is what our Lord noted of John in Chapter 11 of Matthew: *Amen, I say to you, among those born of women there has been none greater than John the Baptist; yet the least in the kingdom of heaven is greater than he.*

That message tells us that we will have to be satisfied during our life on earth in not reaching the perfection of faith that is a reward for those who are in his Kingdom. But, at the same time, it is a message that should motivate us to lead a life that will lead us to his Kingdom.

From the time of Jesus and those who he indicated as having great faith, let us move to contemporary times and examine the faith qualities of people our Church has found worthy to be named saints.

One of my favorite saints of not just contemporary times but of all times is Saint John Paul II. His life was one dedicated to serving our Lord and understanding such service needed to be accompanied by humility. It is sometimes said that our Church serves three main functions: 1 – Adoration 2- Evangelization 3- Serving the poor. In my view, Saint John Paul II performed these three functions as well as they can be performed.

When one reads available biographical information about Saint Paul II, it increases the spiritual respect he so richly deserves. All such information addresses the many hours he would spend in adoration of our Lord. His evangelization efforts were well known. He was especially involved with younger generations. His concerns for the poor have also been well-documented. It seems that every hour of his life was dedicated to the service of our Lord. He was indeed a spiritual role model for all of us to follow.

Another great saint of contemporary times was St. Teresa of Calcutta. The work of Mother Teresa, who was born in Albania, is known around the world. Her work to help the poor in Kolkata (Calcutta) inspired many others to join her Missionaries of Charity. Their work included aiding people with AIDS, leprosy, tuberculosis, and other diseases.

By 1996, the Missionaries of Charity operated more than five hundred missions in over one hundred countries. By that time, the Order also numbered thousands of members, who were serving the "poorest of the poor."

In her private life, Mother Teresa often experienced doubts about her religious beliefs. She often expressed that she had an "emptiness and darkness" in her relationship with God. Those doubts did not prevent her from a lifetime of serving the poorest among us. She served as a role model for all of us in caring for the poor and as a model she attracted many women to join the Missionaries of Charity, who continue doing exemplary work among the poor.

While this chapter was first being drafted, the world learned of the death of Pope Benedict XVI. He was a man of deep faith, wisdom, and holiness. By nature, he was a shy man and that together with his often candid and frank manner of speaking could be offsetting to some. But in my view the words spoken of him as being a "Giant of Faith and Reason" describe him very well. He deserves to be noted in this chapter.

In this chapter, we have chosen only a few people who lived on earth and are examples of those who arrived at or near the apex of faith. All of us are sinners (the Blessed Mother excepted) and as our Lord said of John the Baptist; the greatest among us are not equal to the least in His Kingdom. Nevertheless, those noted in this chapter, along with many other saints, can serve as our role models as we strive to reach the apex of faith.

WISDOM

CHAPTER 5

SPIRITUAL WISDOM
DEFINED

Webster's New World Dictionary defines "Wisdom" as the power of judging rightly and following the soundest course of action, based on knowledge, experience, understanding, etc. Some years ago, I authored a book titled, "The Wisdom of our Soul". As noted in that book the definition provided by Webster is fine when viewed from a secular perspective. Because that definition falls short of defining wisdom from a spiritual perspective, my writings usually refer to "spiritual wisdom" because it is our Lord who provides us with "the soundest course of action." That is an important distinction.

Human wisdom relates to our earthly flesh and is very useful to us in earthly matters. But spiritual wisdom is given to us by God and thus relates to our soul and is of great importance to us as we pursue the Path to Paradise.

It is also easy to confuse human intelligence with spiritual wisdom. Human intelligence is not an indicator of spiritual wisdom. There are many people who by human standards are very intelligent but are severely lacking in spiritual wisdom. There are also people with outstanding spiritual wisdom who do not necessarily possess great human intelligence. Human intelligence is a product of the human brain. Spiritual wisdom is related more to our soul.

Spiritual Wisdom is the first of the seven gifts of the Holy Spirit. It is at the core of continuing growth in faith while we live on this earth. It precedes the second listed Holy Spirit's gift of spiritual understanding and is a necessity to gain such understanding.

In looking to Sacred Scripture to support the definition of spiritual wisdom as provided above, it is useful to turn to St. Paul's letter to the Galatians in which he makes very strong distinctions between the human body and soul:

I say, then: live by the Spirit and you will certainly not gratify the desire of the flesh. For the flesh has desires against the Spirit, and the Spirit against the flesh; these are opposed to each other, so that you may not do what you want. But if you are guided by the Spirit, you are not under the law. Now the works of the flesh are obvious: immorality, impurity, licentiousness, idolatry, sorcery, hatreds, rivalry, jealousy outbursts of fury, acts of selfishness, dissensions, factions, occasions of envy, drinking bouts, orgies, and the like. I warn you as I warned you before, that those who do such things will not inherit the kingdom of God. In contrast, the fruit of the Spirit is love, joy, peace, patience, kindness, generosity, faithfulness, gentleness, self-control. Against such there is no law. Now those who belong to Christ have crucified their flesh with its passions and desires. If we live in the Spirit, let us also follow the Spirit. Let us not be conceited, provoking one another, envious of one another.

St. Paul makes it very clear that it is our flesh (body) that is prone to sinful actions and thoughts, whereas the spiritual wisdom of our soul leads us along the Path to Paradise. As St. Paul notes the flesh and Spirit are often opposed. In such moments, our human brain becomes the arbiter of our thoughts and actions. It is important to all of us that we utilize the discipline required to follow the dictates of our spiritual wisdom emanating from the soul.

The Old Testament provided important insights into spiritual wisdom. These insights are provided throughout the Books of the Old Testament which are referred to as the Wisdom Books. The beginning of Sirach, one of the Wisdom Books, makes it clear that God is the source of spiritual wisdom. "All wisdom comes from the Lord and with him it remains forever." It goes on to say, "To whom has wisdom's roots been revealed? Who knows her subtleties? There is but one, wise and truly awe inspiring, seated upon his throne; It is the Lord."

We need to be humble in how we define our own spiritual wisdom. We must constantly remind ourselves that it is a gift of God and not a trait of human intelligence. We must also be humble because as flawed human beings who sin, there are times when we reject spiritual wisdom and sin. To grow in spiritual wisdom requires spiritual exercises whereas growing in human intelligence depends on gaining earthly knowledge. As noted earlier in this chapter, they are different. and their growth requires different disciplines; one spiritual and the other earthly.

It is important for all of us that we properly define and understand spiritual wisdom and the spiritual disciplines required to grow spiritually. To know spiritual wisdom better is to know God better and hence it is foundational to the Path to Paradise.

We will close this chapter with the beautiful words regarding spiritual wisdom from the Book of Proverbs: *Happy the man who finds wisdom, the man who gains understanding! For her profit is better than profit in silver, and better than gold is her revenue; She is more precious than corals, and none of your choice possessions can compare with her.* To those words we say, AMEN.

CHAPTER 6

THE ACCEPTANCE OF TRUTH

"I am the Way, and the Truth and the Life." Those words by our Lord in John 14:6 were made in response to the Apostle Thomas' comment that we do not know where our Lord is going and how can we know the way to follow Him.

Our Lord's response to Thomas seems simple enough but it is not. The seeds of the Sower fall in many places and for them to bear fruit requires that we accept that our Lord truly is the Way, and the Truth and the Life. That demands that we are willing to accept his Words if we wish to grow in faith and in spiritual wisdom.

To grow in spiritual wisdom requires that we believe the words our sponsors said on our behalf when we were baptized shortly after our birth. In the vows answered by are sponsors, we renounce Satan and all his works. They were the words we also restated at the Confirmation of our faith. It is a necessity to accept Truth by accepting the words of the Bible and of our Catholic Catechism. Without such acceptance, growing in spiritual wisdom is difficult and maybe impossible.

Total faith in the Truth is the key to growing in spiritual wisdom. Once we accept the Way, and the Truth and the Life in totality, we can begin the climb toward the apex of faith. We cannot grow in spiritual wisdom without such acceptance of faith. To deny any Truth provided us in Sacred Scripture or the faith and moral truths of our Catechism, is to deny ourselves the opportunity to grow in spiritual wisdom. We cannot learn to discern what we do not believe, or which we doubt.

To aid us in establishing the foundations of our faith, we need to familiarize ourselves with the teachings contained in Sacred Scripture and the Catechism. It is important to begin the teachings of our faith at an early age. That teaching has been lacking in recent years and has resulted in less acceptance of our faith, which in turn leads to less participation in our faith. Too many today say that youngsters can make up their own mind regarding faith as they grow older. That unfortunately does not work. It may be that faith grows more as reasoning powers mature, but without the basic knowledge of the Truth, it is impossible to grow in spiritual wisdom.

St. Paul taught us that we cannot expect people to understand that which they have not been taught, and that is as true today as it was when St. Paul proclaimed it. If our Catholic Church expects greater participation in the Catholic faith, it needs to redevelop a systematic method of teaching the tenets of our faith. That is sadly lacking at this time.

Our Church tells us early in the Catechism of the Catholic Church that what we have just described is "the obedience of faith." By acceptance of faith and obedience to faith we humans submit our intellect and our will to God. When we speak of The Truth, we are submitting "freely to the word that has been heard from God, because its truth is guaranteed by God, who is Truth." When we accept the Truth and remain faithful to the Truth, we remain among the seed that the Sower planted on fertile ground.

When we do not accept the Word of God (the Truth) we stray from the Path to Paradise. By not believing in the totality of the Word of God we also subject ourselves to being among the seeds that fall on bad ground. We also lose the ability to grow in faith and wisdom. The acceptance of Truth is foundational to growing in faith and wisdom.

As noted earlier, there are too many today who choose not to accept the totality of the Word of God. Surveys indicate that only about 30% of those who claim to be of the Catholic faith practice their faith. That is ignoring the third commandment, which tells us to keep holy the sabbath. The lack of practice of a person's faith also limits the ability to grow in faith and spiritual wisdom.

Today, we also have many Catholics who do not believe in the Real Presence of the Holy Eucharist. Denying the Real Presence is also a denial of the Truth. The Holy Eucharist is the sum and summary of our Catholic faith and to deny the Real Presence also limits our ability to grow our faith and spiritual wisdom. The linkage of humanity and divinity in Holy Communion is in and of itself a grace that helps us grow in spiritual wisdom. More of that reasoning will be included in a later chapter.

There are many reasons cited for the lack of participation in the Catholic faith and in the belief of the Real Presence, but there is more and more indication that the fault is due to a lack of knowledge of Catholic doctrine. As noted earlier, with better teaching of the Catholic faith at an earlier age those faults can be corrected.

CHAPTER 7

SPIRITUAL REASONING

When this book was first begun, the name of this chapter was simply titled "Reasoning." But as I began writing this section of the book, I came to the belief that the word reasoning alone is inadequate to define the gift from God that helps us grow in faith and wisdom. Human reasoning is a process of our human brain that helps us to think logically and analytically to arrive at conclusions drawn from known or assumed facts. That, however, is an incomplete definition for the reasoning we receive as a gift from God. It is that gift that is necessary to be able to reason spiritually and therefore the addition of the word spiritual to the name of this chapter.

Secular wisdom and secular reasoning are both helpful to us in earthly matters. But, if we wish to grow in faith and wisdom, it is a necessity that we have the gift of spiritual reasoning to help us accomplish that goal. Spiritual reasoning is aided by our closeness to

God who is the source of such reasoning. I believe this distinction is important to better understand what we proclaim as faith and reason in order to grow spiritually.

Human reasoning need not be in conflict with spiritual reasoning. We should strive to have a cooperation of the two. Through our free will and intellect, we are able to submit our faith and reasoning to the grace God has given us and thereby assent to The Truth as God has revealed. God has also provided us with physical evidence via his creations, miracles of Jesus and other saints that He is the Way, the Truth, and The Life. And by the grace God has given us we are able to use that spiritual reasoning to ascend the Path to Paradise.

In our Catechism the Church explains this submission to God's revelations as follows: *Human intelligence is surely already capable of finding a response to the question of origins. The existence of God the Creator can be known with certainty through his works, by the light of human reason, even if this knowledge is often obscured and disfigured by error. This is why faith comes to confirm and enlighten reason in the correct understanding of this truth: "By faith we understand that the world was created by the word of God, so that what is seen was made out of things which do not appear."*

As is true of faith, there also great mystery surrounding spiritual reasoning. Medical science has told us that human thinking or reasoning is performed by the frontal lobe of the cerebral cortex with involvement from the parietal lobes. That applies to the definition of human reasoning alone. How such reasoning is supplemented by the grace of God to cooperate with his gift of spiritual reasoning is mysterious. It is also mysterious as to how spiritual reasoning may continue in the absence of human reasoning.

During our time on earth many of us are afflicted with Alzheimer's disease or dementia. We understand that they, along with accidents affecting the cerebral cortex, prohibit or diminish human reasoning. Do they also diminish spiritual reasoning? We do not know exactly how the grace of God's gift is affected by damage to human reasoning. We have had examples of people who have been in accidents and comas who seem to have experienced life after death.

It is also a mystery as to what spiritual reasoning God may bestow upon us in life hereafter. We simply do not know what such reasoning may be. It seems logical that some form of such reasoning would be a part of life after death, if we are to understand the judgments God will bestow on us. Without some form of reasoning such judgments would be meaningless but we simply do not know what such reasoning may be.

Since this book deals with the Path to Paradise during this life, let us return to the value of spiritual reasoning during our time on earth. Our Church in paragraph 158 of the CCC informs us that "Faith Seeks Understanding". If we have faith in God, it should be our desire to better know Him. Through God's gift of spiritual reasoning, we are able to do that. Our Church refers to this desire as "a lively understanding of the contents of Revelation; that is, of the totality of God's plan and the mysteries of faith, of their connection with each other and with Christ, the center of revealed mystery."

As we grow in faith and spiritual wisdom, it will be our desire with the help of the Holy Spirit to better understand what God has revealed. That is where spiritual reasoning comes to our assistance. St. Augustine put it very well with his words, "I believe, in order to understand; and I understand, the better to believe." It should be a daily prayer for us to have the Holy Spirit, through the use of our spiritual reasoning, assist us to better understand. We are also aided in that pursuit through prayer, spiritual study, and other spiritual activities.

The pursuit of greater faith and the utilization of spiritual reasoning must be lifetime pursuits if we wish to ascend the Path to Paradise. If we stray from that Path, we are in danger of being seed that has not fallen on fertile ground. As we make it a part of our daily life to better understand, the Holy Spirit will continue to provide us with the spiritual reasoning power needed.

CHAPTER 8

SPIRITUAL UNDERSTANDING

As we noted earlier, The Book of Proverbs tells us that blessed is the man who finds wisdom and gains understanding.

Spiritual understanding is the second gift of the Holy Spirit. It is preceded only by the gift of wisdom. They are important to each other. Spiritual wisdom has been defined as the desire to better understand and contemplate the things of God, whereas spiritual understanding is the gift that permits us to know and penetrate those things of God.

Pope Francis has noted that the gift of understanding helps us to move closer to understand things as God understands them.

When starting this chapter, I asked my wife how she would define spiritual understanding. Her answer was a very succinct "closeness to God."

Let us then move on to the ways we can better understand and become closer to the things of God. Since there are different ways we can become closer to the things of God, let me state early that these are some of my own personal views. I believe to better understand the things of God involves our better understanding of the role of each Person of the Blessed Trinity.

In thinking and appreciating the magnificence and omnipotence of God the Father, I am very rapidly drawn to the splendor of His Domain. In our Nicene Creed, we are very brief in the words dedicated to the Father: *I believe in one God, the Father Almighty, maker of heaven and earth, of all things visible and invisible.* The words may be brief but say so very much.

When I think of God the Father, the word Almighty and all his works quickly come to mind. What we humans can observe is extremely limited but should lead us to appreciate Him as maker of all things, visible and invisible. As science has progressed, we have been made more aware of the millions of galaxies that exist and have been created from nothing by the maker of all things. Sadly, many in this world reject Him as maker of all things, but I can only repeat what St. Paul noted in his Letter to the Romans. They are fools.

As we spend time attributing all creation to our Heavenly Father, we can ponder the magnificence and immeasurability of those creations. They are beyond the comprehension of our human brain, but with the Holy Spirit's gift of understanding we can appreciate such splendor. We can dwell at length on the infinity of

He who also is not only the maker of all things visible and invisible, but also the master of infinite space and time. As science progresses, it will undoubtedly discover more of his magnificent creations.

My favorite song of praise, Holy God, is often sung at the close of holy hours and Benediction. As we close the first stanza we proudly and adoringly proclaim "Infinite they vast Domain and everlasting is they Reign".

From God the Father, we come to God the Son. In my morning and evening prayers I include a special thank you to each Person of the Blessed Trinity. I begin that with a thank you to the Father for the magnificence of his creations. To the Son I say thank you for your great love demonstrated by your passion and death on the Cross to redeem our sins. There is no greater love.

Jesus Christ came to earth in a very humble manner. He was born in a stable and worked with Joseph as a carpenter prior to his public years. He is a model for us to be humble. But more than anything else, He is our model of the meaning of love. He came to earth as our Teacher and revealed to us the Way, the Truth and the Life. He not only came to earth as the Teacher of Love, but He came to earth to demonstrate that love through his passion and death. Through that passion and death, we have become the adopted children of our Heavenly Father. He made it possible to spend our eternal life in his Kingdom.

We could go on at great length with He who taught us the Way, the Truth, and the Life. Our language lacks the superlatives to describe He who died for us. So we will simply end our description of our Lord and Master by echoing the words our Catechism uses in paragraph 520. *In all of his life Jesus presents himself as our model. He is "the perfect man", who invites us to become his disciples and follow him. In humbling himself, he has given us an example to imitate, through his prayer he draws us to pray, and by his poverty he calls us to accept freely the privation and persecutions that may come our way.*

For He who died for us, it is a worthwhile practice to spend a part of each day reading Scriptures and studying our Catechism. By knowing Him better through those practices, we will also be able to love Him more and help us ascend the Path to Paradise, where He resides in glory.

Lastly, we come to the Third Person of the Blessed Trinity, the Holy Spirit. As is true of God the Father, the Nicene Creed is also fairly brief in speaking of the Holy Spirit. It simply states; *I believe in the Holy Spirit, the Lord, the giver of life, who proceeds from the Father and the Son, who with the Father and the Son is adored and glorified, who has spoken through the prophets.* While being brief, it also tells us much.

In my morning and evening prayers, I thank the Holy Spirit for his constant spiritual guidance. I often refer to the Holy Spirit as my Spiritual Director. He is with me constantly to keep me on the Path to Paradise. Because I am a sinner, my flesh strays from the Path, but the Holy Spirit brings me back if I repent for having strayed.

Our Church tell us that through His grace, the

Holy Spirit is the first to awaken faith in us and to communicate to us that new life which is as John in Chapter 17 communicates to us; "know the Father and the one whom he has sent, Jesus Christ".

The Holy Spirit is a special gift to us from God. Our Catechism explains that as follows: *"God is Love" and love is his first gift, containing all others. "God's love has been poured into our hearts through the Holy Spirit who has been given to us.* If all of us on earth were more attentive to the prompts of the Holy Spirit within us, we would stray less from the Path to Paradise.

While speaking of the Holy Spirit, this is a suitable time to inform my readers that, in my writings, I rarely speak of the spirit as a part of me but rather I generally speak of humans being comprised of a body and soul. My reason for doing that is my own belief that it is the Holy Spirit who is a constant companion as opposed to being a part of me.

Spiritual understanding will lead us to spending our time on things God wants us to do with our time on earth. And part of that time should always include spiritual efforts to better understanding of He who made us. Better understanding leads to greater love of Him who is love and as noted love is his first gift. All the other gifts, including those of the Holy Spirit are given to us to love Him all the more.

HOLINESS

CHAPTER 9

PRAYER

As we achieve spiritual wisdom and understanding we will also have the desire to live a holy life. Holiness is the achievement of excellence in our moral and spiritual life. There are numerous ways to achieve holiness. The most common way is through prayer. Frequent prayer is a necessity to ascend the Path to Paradise.

Prayer is a universal activity for people of many religions. For Christians, it is a method of moral and spiritual communications between humans and God. Prayer is not only an activity involving humans' communications to God but also includes listening to God's words.

St. Therese of Lisieux had a beautiful personal description of prayer. "For me prayer is a surge of the heart; it is a simple look turned toward heaven. It is a cry of recognition and of love, embracing both trial and joy". St. John Damascene described it a little differently.

"Prayer is the raising of one's mind and heart to God or the requesting of good things from God". Our Church reminds us that according to Scripture, prayer comes from the heart and if our heart is far from God, the words of prayer are in vain.

In the last chapter, we noted that spiritual understanding means a closeness to God. The same can be said for prayer. To pray from the heart is to put ourselves in the presence of our God.

The Bible tells us that Jesus prayed often. He also taught us the words to pray and how to pray when he gave his Sermon on the Mount. In Chapter 6:9-13 of Matthew, Jesus gave us those beautiful words of the "Lord's Prayer" or "Our Father" which are repeated at every Catholic Mass.

There are a number of different forms of prayer. Blessing is the most basic form. The Catechism describes it as "an encounter between God and man". It goes on to tell us that the prayer of blessing is man's response to God's gifts, which are His blessings to us.

Adoration is also a basic form of prayer. In prayers of Adoration, we acknowledge that we are the creatures of our Creator and in Adoration we exalt and glorify Him who created us and all things and who loves us. During the Mass, the Gloria is often said and is referred to as the Angelic Hymn. In the Catholic Church we often have extended times as well as holy hours of special Adoration. Such Adoration is one of the highest forms of prayer. We will include a separate chapter on

Adoration as we believe it to be an important aspect of Holiness. It will continue to be that in Paradise.

One of the most common forms of prayer is for Petition and at the top of the list of Petitions is asking for forgiveness. Our petition to Him for forgiveness and mercy is our turning point in receiving his mercy and returning us to the state of grace. Prayers of petition include our needs to one day be with Him in Paradise.

Prayers of Intercession are another form of prayer. Through prayers of Intercession, we ask our Lord to provide for others their needs. In praying for others, we also perform an act of kindness on their behalf. Our Lord reminded us that it is also good to pray for our enemies. There are no boundaries on those for whom we pray.

Another form of prayer is Prayer of Thanksgiving. We receive countless blessings from our Lord and Savior for which we should be thankful frequently. His suffering and death on the Cross made our salvation possible and that alone should be reason for daily Thanksgiving. From a personal standpoint, a good time to be thankful is during Adoration.

Finally, we have Prayers of Praise, whereby we simply praise Him for being our God. Our Church in the Catechism notes that through Prayers of Praise we praise Him because "He Is". It goes on to note that in Prayers of Praise, we praise the "one God, the Father, from whom are all things and for whom we exist".

Our Church also notes three Expressions (methods) of Prayer. Before reviewing those, Jesus told us how we are to pray in Matthew 6: 5-8: *When you pray, do not be like the hypocrites, who love to stand and pray in the synagogues and on street corners so that others may see them. Amen, I say to you, they have received their reward. But when you pray, go to your inner room, close the door and pray to your Father in secret. And your Father who sees in secret will repay you. In praying, do not babble like the pagans, who think they will be heard because of their many words. Do not be like them. Your Father knows what you need before you ask him.*

Let us now look at the "Expressions of Prayer" our Church notes in the Catechism. The first is Vocal Prayers which are an important part of Christian life. Jesus taught his disciples a vocal prayer, the Our Father. When we gather in Church or in groups, vocal prayer is that which is most accessible.

The second expression of prayer is Meditation. Through Meditation we seek to understand the why and how of Christian life, and thereby we respond to what the Lord is asking. In Meditation we are often aided by spiritual reading, especially the Sacred Scriptures. There is also the Catechism and other spiritual readings to aid us. It is good to meditate frequently, because it is a great aid to help us deepen our faith.

The third and very important expression of prayer is Contemplation. St. Teresa of Avila described such prayer very aptly and succinctly when she explained it as follows: *Contemplative Prayer in my opinion is nothing else than a close sharing between friends; it means taking time frequently to be alone with him who we know loves us.* I find that description to be very complete.

In my personal life I find a good place for contemplative prayer to be practiced is in the quiet of my room as Jesus suggested we pray to the Father. Another very good time to be contemplative is the quiet period during Adoration, when I am in the Lord's presence. It is an intense time of prayer as it should be when we are in "a close sharing between friends" and in this case with our very best friend, our Lord and Savior.

As noted at the beginning of this chapter, prayer is an activity that is practiced by people of many religions. But as is true of faith, prayer can also be viewed as a spiritual battle. Our prayers are often interrupted by distractions, and we can also experience periods of "dryness" as well as other situations we view as failures in our praying. These "failures" can be treated as acts of humility by recognizing them as our human failings.

There are some fairly common reasons for prayer distractions. The place where we pray can be a distraction. A Church or chapel is the best place for praying as we are surrounded by the tabernacle and other spiritual reminders. If most of our prayers are at home, we can reduce the distractions by having crucifixes, statues, or other spiritual icons in the place we most frequently pray. It is unlikely that sports arenas, movie theaters or other such places that are used for non-prayerful events are good places to visit for the purpose of praying.

Distractions also come from other matters related to things of this world, work, people, events, to-dos, etc. It is good to specifically schedule our prayer time during the day, in order to better focus on prayer during those times. To do things of this world is necessary for our livelihood, but scheduling ourselves for prayer time and things of God is to keep on The Path to Paradise.

All of us on earth experience distractions, dryness, and other failures in praying. Our Catholic Catechism advises us that these failures need to be battled with humility, trust in God and perseverance. Our Lord understands our human weaknesses and is pleased when we repent and return to praying to Him. In John 15: 5 our Lord reminds us that "Whoever remains in me and I in him will bear much fruit, because without me you can do nothing." These are good words to help us persevere in praying.

Despite the difficulties we may encounter in our prayer efforts, praying is important to our Christian life. St. John Chrysostom reminded us that it is always possible to pray. He told us that prayer is possible "while walking in public or strolling alone or seated in your shop…while buying or selling…or even while cooking."

Prayer is a necessity for all Christians. Prayer and Christian life are inseparable. God is love and in praying we express our love of Him. We will conclude this chapter with words from Origen, an early Christian scholar and theologian; He *"prays without ceasing" who unites prayer to works and good works to prayer. Only in this way can we consider as realizable the principle of praying without ceasing."*

Those words of Origen will also lead us to our next chapter on good works.

CHAPTER 10

LOVE OF NEIGHBOR AND GOOD WORKS

Our Lord himself told us that doing good works is a by-product of our faith in Him. In John 14: 12, Jesus tells us "Amen, amen I say to you, whoever believes in me will do the works that I do, and will do greater ones than these, because I am going to the Father".

As Origen noted and our Lord confirmed, good works are united with faith and prayer. When our Lord spoke of works "greater than these" He obviously was not talking of miracles or other divine powers. In my view, He was telling us that with faith in Him, we could proclaim The Way, The Truth, and The Life to many others. He did much in His three years of public life and those who believe in Him can bring His words to many more on earth. I do believe His words spoke to the importance of salvation, which is what He was addressing at the beginning of the 14th chapter of John.

Jesus, during his time on earth also spoke of aiding others through good works that do relate to earthly works as opposed to the heavenly works He spoke to in Verse 12 of Chapter 14. But He did place the highest priority of good works on the salvation of souls. That seems spiritually logical to me, because the salvation of our soul speaks to our purpose on earth and eternal holiness.

But we cannot love our Lord if we do not love our neighbor. In the first letter of John 4:20 we are provided the message of the importance of loving our neighbor: *If anyone says, "I love God" but hates his brother, he is a liar; for whoever does not love a brother whom he has seen cannot love God whom he has not seen. This is the commandment we have from him: whoever loves God must also love his brother.*

As Origen noted, good works are united with faith and prayer. For me, there is also a linkage of faith, prayer, good works, and love of neighbor. Our Lord's two great commandments that we love Him with all our heart, soul, mind and strength and our neighbor as ourself, for me also implies the linkage just noted. But the words of our Lord clearly notes that such linkage begins with faith in Him. And that linkage makes our Lord's word "works" very broad. For all humans his works are the vocation of humanity.

Our Church in pp 1877 of the Catechism states the vocation of humanity as follows: *The vocation of humanity is to show forth the image of God and to be transformed into the image of the Father's only Son. This vocation takes a personal form since each of us is called to enter into the divine beatitude; it also concerns the human community as a whole.*

If each of us on earth would do the works as our Lord would have us do them, we would have the words fulfilled we pray for in the Our Father: Thy Kingdom come, thy will be done. God has endowed all humans with talents that vary a great deal and thus we contribute to society in different ways. But the one single vocation we have during our time on earth is to conduct our lives in a manner that is pleasing to our Creator.

When I began this chapter, it was my intent to list some of the good works that can be performed by individuals but that inevitably leads to missing some that should have been noted. Instead of doing that, it is probably better to merely state that by doing acts that are of benefit to our neighbor or society we are also performing acts that are pleasing to God. The foundation for such good works is faith in God which leads us to love of Him, neighbor, and performance of good works.

God has not reserved to himself the exercise of all power. He entrusts to us humans many functions which we are capable of performing and He has given individuals a variety of talents to make such functions possible for them. When those functions are done for the benefit of society we are doing "good works".

When all members of society observe our Lord's command to love our neighbor as ourselves, we achieve a high level of social justice. In fulfilling social justice demands, it is important to serve those who are disadvantaged in some way. Our Church tells us that the same duty extends to those who think or act differently, including those of diverse cultural backgrounds. God is the Father to all of us on earth, and it is important that we treat everyone as our brother or sister.

For those who are disadvantaged economically, it is our duty to treat them charitably and thereby reduce excessive social and economic inequalities. Love of neighbor demands our generosity.

Good works also include the care of the world we live in. It is important that all human beings not only love their neighbor, but also all of God's creation, including our earth. In loving God's creation of this earth, we need to treat it as He would want us to treat it. That means leaving this earth as good or better than we found it. While on that subject, I think it is also good for all of us to understand that our Lord is also the master of this universe including the climate. All too often we forget nature's God and ignore his power over the climate.

In closing this chapter, we remember that love of neighbor and good works are best accomplished when we live humbly before our Lord and others and when we practice the virtues of kindness and charity.

CHAPTER 11

THE HOLY EUCHARIST

The Catholic Church refers to the Holy Eucharist as the Source and Summit of Ecclesial life. It also refers to it as the Sum and Summary of our Faith. Our Church teaches us that by the consecration of the bread and wine there takes place a change of the whole substance of the bread into the substance of the body of Christ our Lord and of the whole substance of the wine into the substance of his blood. The Church calls this change transubstantiation. Sadly, many Christians, including a significant percentage of Catholic do not believe in the "Real Presence" of our Lord, in the Eucharist.

There are many miracles and mysteries surrounding our faith in God. Some of those include the creation of the universe by God from nothing. To that we can add the birth of our Lord to a virgin. The resurrection of our Lord can be added to the list of miracles and mysteries the human mind can accept but not fully understand.

Why the "Real Presence" seems to be more difficult to accept by Christians is a mystery to this writer. Having accepted the belief in the "Real Presence" since my very youthful age, it does not necessarily seem to me that the "Real Presence" is more difficult to accept than the other mysteries noted in this paragraph.

Despite this writer's lack of understanding regarding those who cannot accept the "Real Presence," our Church recognizes that difficulty and explains it in CCC 1336 of the Catholic Catechism as follows:

The first announcement of the Eucharist divided the disciples just as the announcement of the Passion scandalized them: "This is a hard saying, who can listen to it?" The Eucharist and the Cross are stumbling blocks. It is the same mystery and it never ceases to be an occasion of division. "Will you also go away?" the Lord's question echoes through the ages, as a loving invitation to discover that only he has the "words of eternal life" and that to receive in faith the gift of his Eucharist is to receive the Lord himself.

It is sad that such a small percentage of Christians believe in the "Real Presence", because it truly is the sum and summary of our faith. It links our humanity with the divinity of our Lord. In doing that we provide spiritual nourishment to our soul. That spiritual nourishment helps us to grow in spiritual wisdom and understanding. It is also the greatest act of holiness on earth.

There have been changes in the way Catholic Doctrine has been taught in the past 60 years. For reasons that are difficult to understand the Baltimore

Catechism, which was the pillar of teaching our faith to our youth, was discontinued. It was also not replaced by another Catechism for teaching purposes. When St. John Paul II released the Catechism of the Catholic Church, he requested that it be used as a sure text for teaching the Catholic faith. He also requested that compendia be prepared. Such a compendium has never been prepared for teaching our elementary school students. I can only contribute such neglect to diabolical intrusion. How much the lack of teaching correct Catholic doctrine has to do with the low percentage of those believing in the "Real Presence" is debatable, but in my view, it is a significant factor.

At about the same time that the Baltimore Catechism was discontinued the number of religious teaching Catholic youth was also beginning to decline. They played a significant role in the teaching of Catholic doctrine. Without the Catechism and the nuns to teach it, we have had a significant decline in the percentage of Catholics who practice their faith and in those who do not believe in the "Real Presence." Both of those make it much more difficult to reach the apex of The Path to Paradise.

If we wish to reverse the decline noted above, the Church needs to have a better systematic method of teaching the Catholic faith. Two steps would be a significant improvement to what exists at the present time. Step one is to prepare a compendium or compendia for teaching our youth and those wishing to convert to the Catholic religion. Step two is for all Bishops to approve such compendia and instruct all parishes that the approved compendia are to be used for teaching the faith. Why that has not been done seems diabolical. St. Paul noted the problem almost two thousand years ago. You cannot expect people to believe that which they have not been taught.

Faith is a relationship with our Lord. It cannot be taught, but the tenets of our Catholic faith can be taught and without a better and more systematic approach to such teaching, we diminish the opportunity to increase the practice of our Catholic faith and the belief in the "Real Presence."

Such improved teaching of the Catholic faith needs to emphasize that the Holy Eucharist is the sum and summary of our Catholic faith. We will devote the remainder of this chapter to why the Eucharist is the foundation of teaching our Catholic faith.

Vatican II documents noted the importance of the Holy Eucharist to the Church; "The Eucharist shows itself to be the source and summit of the whole proclamation of the Gospel". It went on to state that the Most Blessed Sacrament contains the Church's entire spiritual wealth. Those words alone should be ample for instructing all baptized Catholics in the great spiritual value of the Holy Eucharist. The Church needs to make that better known to all Catholics. Article 3 of the Catechism of the Catholic Church does a beautiful job of explaining the Eucharist and a summation of that Article would provide good material for teaching compendia of the Catechism.

Chapter 6 of the Gospel of John covers our Lord's Bread of Life Discourse. We will now look to that chapter to provide quotes from our Lord regarding the Holy Eucharist: Amen, amen, I say to you, whoever believes has eternal life. I am the bread of life. Your ancestors ate the manna in the desert, but they died; this is the bread that comes down from heaven, so that one may eat it and not die. I am the living bread that came down from heaven; whoever eats this bread will live forever; and the bread that I will give is my flesh for the life of the world.

At that point in the Bread of Life Discourse the Jews quarreled among themselves on how Jesus could give us his flesh to eat. Jesus went on to say; *Amen, amen, I say to you, unless you eat the flesh of the Son of Man and drink his blood, you do not have life within you. Whoever eats my flesh and drinks my blood has eternal life, and I will raise him on the last day.*

Jesus understood that there were many of his disciples who found it impossible to believe His words and Jesus went on to say that the belief was no more impossible than would be his Ascension into heaven from where He came to be with us. The Bread of Life Discourse should provide adequate words from our Lord to have us believe in the "Real Presence".

But the Bread of Life Discourse is not the only reference to our Lord's presence in the Holy Eucharist. On the night before he died, he gathered with his Apostles to share "this Passover" meal with them. In Chapter 22; 19-20 of Luke, our Lord provides additional evidence of the "Real Presence"; *Then he took the bread, said the blessing, broke it and gave it to them saying, "This is my body, which will be given for you; do this in memory of me." And likewise the cup after they had eaten, saying, "This cup is the new covenant in my blood, which will be shed for you.* There are no limitations on the omnipotence of our Lord. It is human limitations of faith that are the cause of disbelief.

It is by our faith that we accept the many miracles disclosed in Sacred Scriptures. Why the miracle of transubstantiation is more difficult to accept than many of the other miracles is difficult for this writer to understand. It may be the miracle performed daily at the Holy Mass is more difficult because it is a miracle of contemporary times, as well as one that has been performed throughout the past two thousand years.

To those who have been given the grace to believe in the "Real Presence", thanksgiving is in order at each Holy Communion. Through the linkage of their humanity with the Body and Blood of our Lord, they have nourishment for their soul. That nourishment is a provider of greater faith, wisdom, understanding and holiness. Our Lord has promised them to be raised up on the last day. In their belief, they have found the apex of The Path to Paradise.

CHAPTER 12

ADORATION

As we noted in the Chapter on Prayer, St. Teresa of Avila referred to contemplative prayer as a close sharing between friends. In my view, her description can also be used to describe Adoration. When we spend an hour or more with our Lord in the exposed monstrance, we are at the apex of The Path to Paradise. It has been written that when we spend time with our Lord in Adoration, we are in the vestibule of Heaven. I very much agree with that view.

When we receive the Holy Eucharist, we are joined in Holy Communion with the Body, Blood, Soul, and Divinity of our Lord. As noted in the prior chapter, our Church refers to the Eucharist as the Source and Summit of Ecclesial life. As such, it is the apex of The Path to Paradise. When we reach that apex, we also have the opportunity to enter into the vestibule of Heaven noted above. It is through Adoration that we can visit quietly with our Lord and spend time with Him in both meditative and contemplative prayer. It is our opportunity to praise and glorify Him for everything He means to us during our life on earth and be closer to Him than anywhere else on earth.

In paragraph 2096 of the Catechism, our Church explains Adoration as follows: *Adoration is the first act of the virtue of religion. To adore God is to acknowledge him as God, as the Creator and Savior, the Lord and Master of everything that exists, as infinite and merciful Love. "You shall worship the Lord your God, and him only shall you serve," says Jesus, citing Deuteronomy.*

When we are in Adoration, we have the opportunity to relate to each person of the Blessed Trinity. Yes, it is a mystery, but all of us probably have our own thoughts on the attributes of each Person of the Trinity. During Adoration we can spend time praising and thanking our Father for His magnificent and splendid domain. His works of creation go far beyond that which we can comprehend. He is the Father who always has been and always will be. Science has now discovered many millions of galaxies and how many exist beyond their discoveries are beyond our understanding.

In Adoration, we can also spend time praising and thanking the second person of the Blessed Trinity, our Savior and Redeemer, Jesus Christ. It is hard to understand how God could humble himself to come to live among us and be born in a humble stable. He would extend that humility into his earthly life and spend his early days on earth as a carpenter. In his three years of public life, He would reveal to us the things we must know to one day enter His Kingdom. It is the Kingdom He would earn for us by his passion and death on a cross.

During Adoration, we can also praise and thank the Holy Spirit for being our Spiritual Director on earth. If we open the ears of our soul, the Holy Spirit provides us with constant spiritual guidance. We are indeed blessed to have Him with us following our Lord's Ascension into Heaven. It is our spiritual duty to praise and thank Him for His spiritual guidance. Our world would be a far better place if each of us listened to His guidance. Through His guidance we can also seek His directions on the good works we can perform during our time on earth.

To adore, praise and thank God is to humble our self before Him to whom we owe our very existence. Such exaltation allows us to turn away from the decay of earthly matters and place Him above all else and properly treat Him as the One who loves us and wants us to love Him. In Adoration we fulfill his commandment to love Him with all our heart, soul, mind, and strength.

St. Alphonsus Liguori said that among all the devotions after that of receiving the Sacraments, adoring Jesus in the Blessed Sacrament, holds first place and is the most pleasing to God and most useful to us. St. Alphonsus suggested all of us make some time available each day to spend time in the presence of the Blessed Sacrament.

During our time before the Blessed Sacrament, it is good and right to adore, praise, glorify and thank

Him. But we can also use such time for other forms of prayer. Our Lord knows what we need before we ask Him, but He loves to hear our prayers of petition and intercession. In doing that we also humble ourselves and acknowledge his greatness and ability to grant our requests.

Adoration time as just noted is also a good time for Prayers of Intercession on behalf of others. Such prayers for help to others are also a form of good works. Our Lord knows better than us the help that others need. In these prayers it is good to remember the poor souls in purgatory and those who are disadvantaged on earth. We can add our prayers that our Lord enlightens those who lead our Church and our governments.

Our Lord welcomes all forms of prayer during our time in Adoration, but it is important to use such time to adore, praise and thank Him for all He does for us as well as all people in our world. In doing that with fervor and ardor, we fulfill his first commandment to love Him with all our heart, soul, mind, and strength.

We conclude this book with the chapters on the Eucharist and on Adoration. It is my belief that we reach the apex of The Path to Paradise when we receive our Lord in the Eucharist. Having reached the apex, we enter the vestibule of Heaven during times of Adoration in His presence in the monstrance.

Our Lord very wisely chose bread as the vehicle for His Real Presence. We need bread on this earth to feed our bodies and we need the Bread from Heaven to nourish our souls. In gazing upon His Real

Presence in the monstrance it is easy to move quickly to contemplative prayer with our Lord and increase our desire to spend eternity with Him who is Love. Such is the power of Adoration, from which we will want to proceed through the doors of the vestibule and enter into Paradise.

ABOUT THE AUTHOR

George E Pfautsch spent most of his working life as a financial executive for a major forest products and paper company. His final years with Potlatch Corporation (now Potlatch Deltic Corporation) were spent as the Senior Vice-President of Finance and Chief Financial Officer.

Following his retirement, he began writing about the national morality he believes was intended for this country by the founding fathers. He is the author of fifteen previous books covering the subjects of faith, freedom, morality, and justice.

In addition, he is the co-author of a book written by Melitta Strandberg, which is the story of her family's quest for freedom, before, during and after World War II. He is also the co-author of a book written by Leroy New, the "Guitar Wizard" of Branson, Missouri.

George is married to Dodi, his wife of more than 60 years. He has two children, four grandchildren and one great-grandchild.

Printed in the United States
by Baker & Taylor Publisher Services